My First Book About Weather

Donald M. Silver &
Patricia J. Wynne

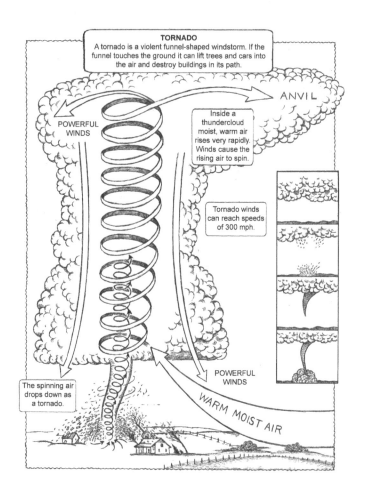

TORNADO
A tornado is a violent funnel-shaped windstorm. If the funnel touches the ground it can lift trees and cars into the air and destroy buildings in its path.

ANVIL

POWERFUL WINDS

Inside a thundercloud moist, warm air rises very rapidly. Winds cause the rising air to spin.

Tornado winds can reach speeds of 300 mph.

POWERFUL WINDS

The spinning air drops down as a tornado.

WARM MOIST AIR

DOVER PUBLICATIONS, INC.
Mineola, New York

For Iancu Sorell
Painter, pianist, philosopher, chef, friend
DMS

Special thanks to Wally Broecker
PJW

Bibliographical Note
My First Book About Weather is a new work,
first published by Dover Publications, Inc., in 2016.

International Standard Book Number
ISBN-13: 978-0-486-79872-1
ISBN-10: 0-486-79872-0

Manufactured in the United States by RR Donnelley
79872001   2016
www.doverpublications.com

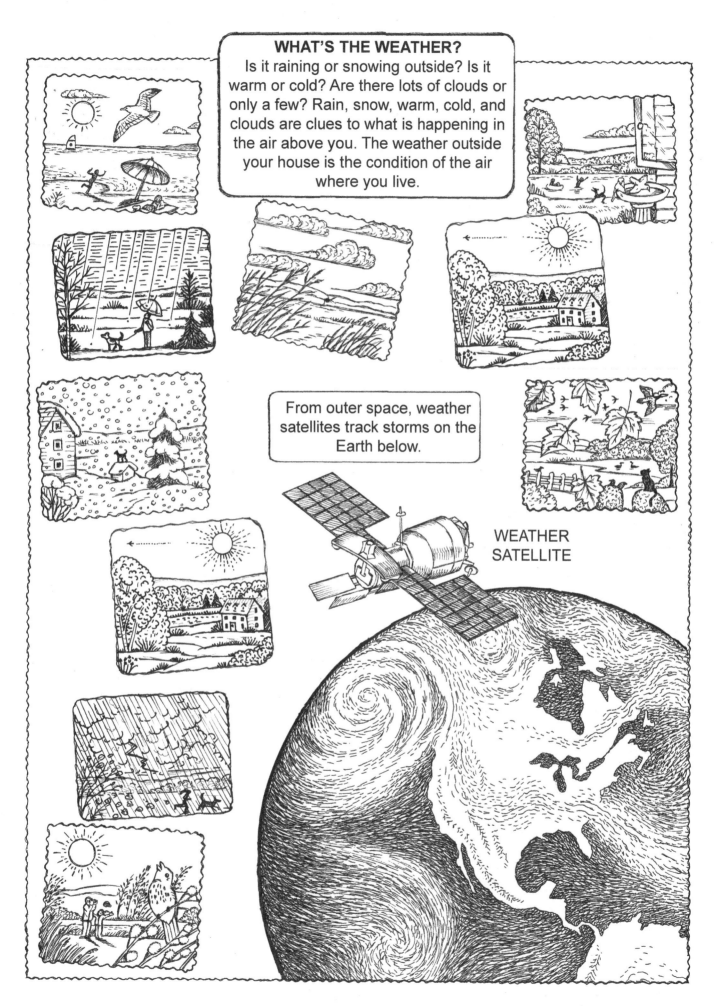

WHAT'S THE WEATHER?
Is it raining or snowing outside? Is it warm or cold? Are there lots of clouds or only a few? Rain, snow, warm, cold, and clouds are clues to what is happening in the air above you. The weather outside your house is the condition of the air where you live.

From outer space, weather satellites track storms on the Earth below.

WEATHER
SATELLITE

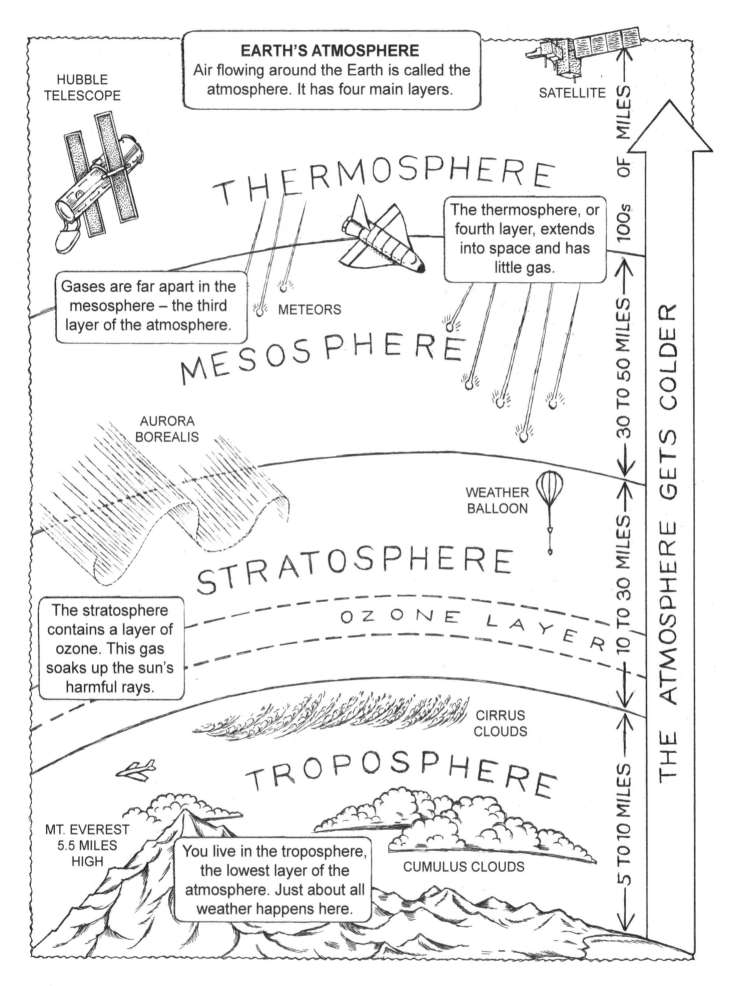

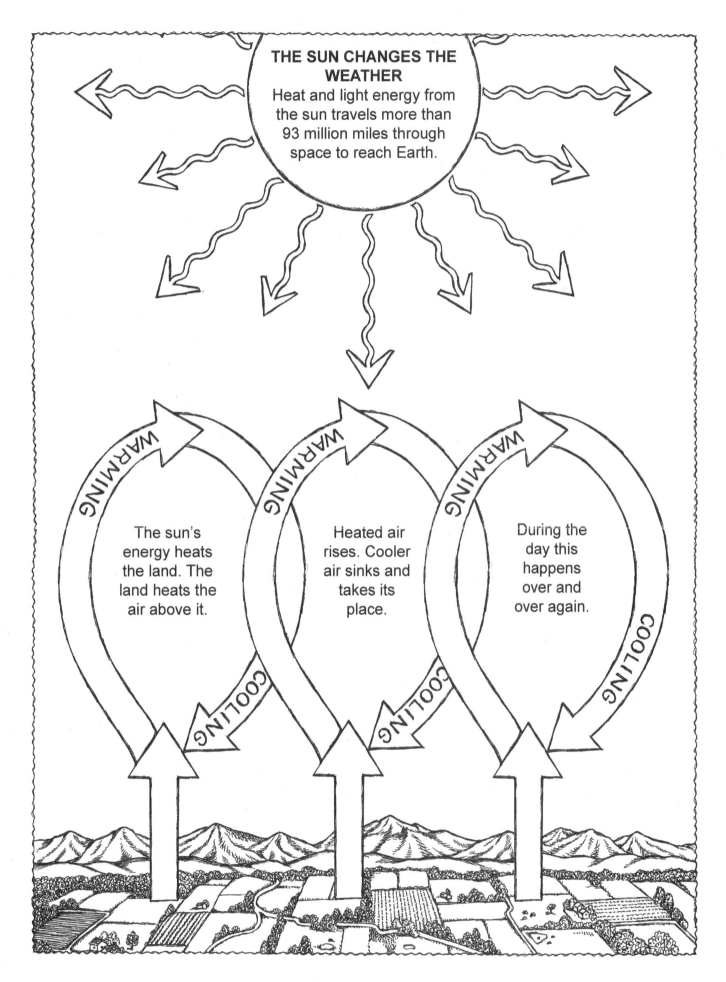

THE SUN CHANGES THE WEATHER
Heat and light energy from the sun travels more than 93 million miles through space to reach Earth.

WARMING

WARMING

WARMING

The sun's energy heats the land. The land heats the air above it.

Heated air rises. Cooler air sinks and takes its place.

During the day this happens over and over again.

COOLING

COOLING

COOLING

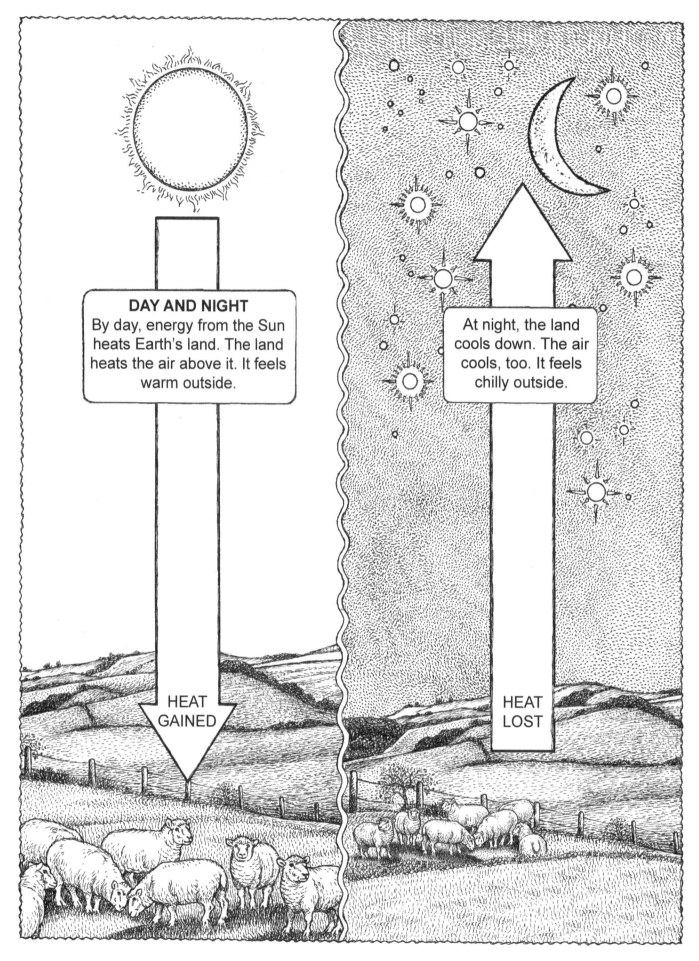

DAY AND NIGHT
By day, energy from the Sun heats Earth's land. The land heats the air above it. It feels warm outside.

At night, the land cools down. The air cools, too. It feels chilly outside.

HEAT GAINED

HEAT LOST

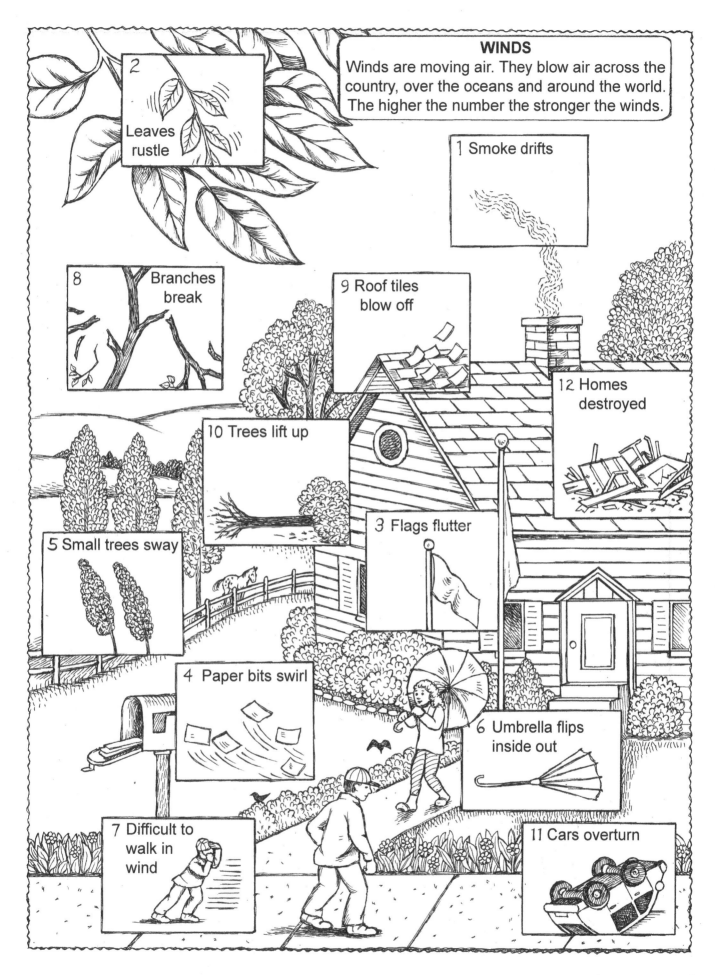

WINDS
Winds are moving air. They blow air across the country, over the oceans and around the world. The higher the number the stronger the winds.

2 Leaves rustle

1 Smoke drifts

8 Branches break

9 Roof tiles blow off

12 Homes destroyed

10 Trees lift up

5 Small trees sway

3 Flags flutter

4 Paper bits swirl

6 Umbrella flips inside out

7 Difficult to walk in wind

11 Cars overturn

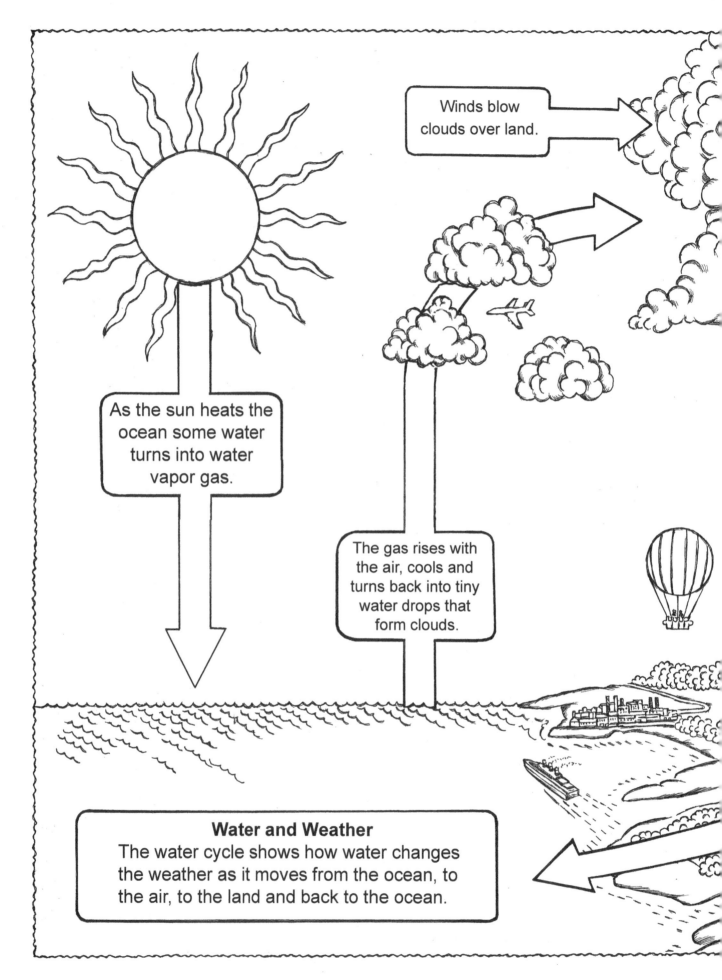

CLOUDS
Billions and billions of tiny floating water drops or ice crystals make up clouds.

Feathery cirrus clouds signal a change in the weather.

White, puffy cumulus clouds mean fair weather.

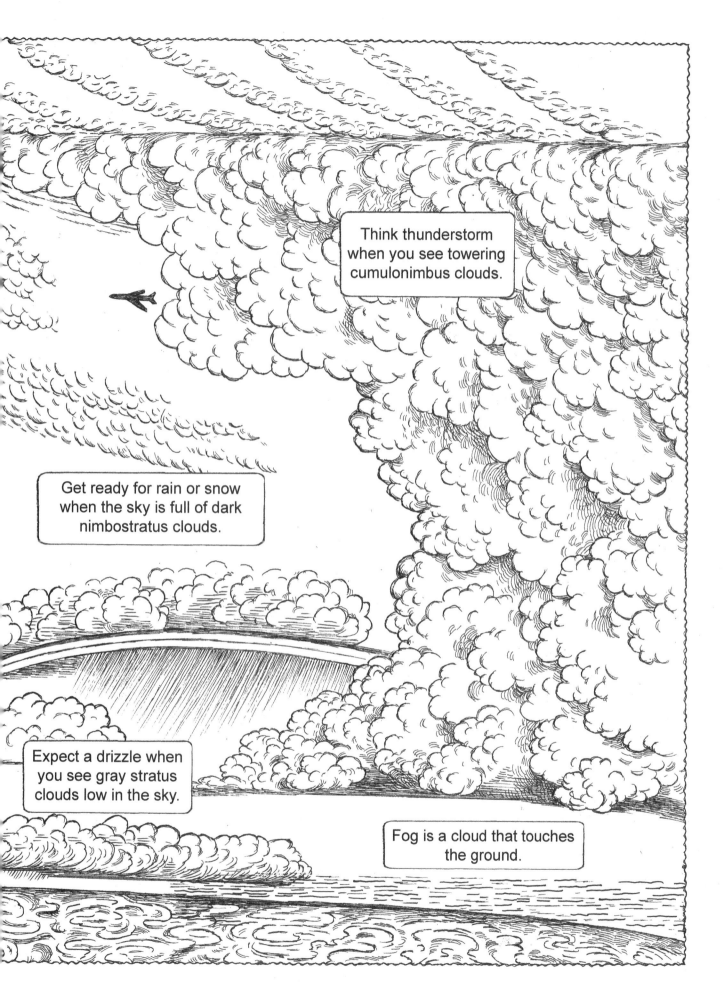

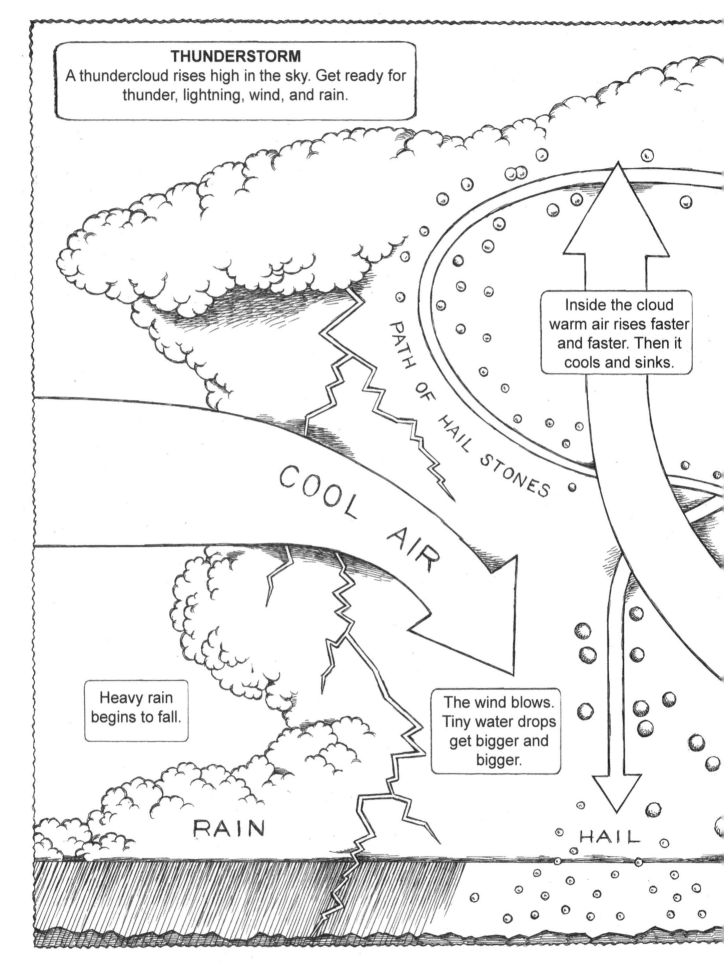

THUNDERSTORM
A thundercloud rises high in the sky. Get ready for thunder, lightning, wind, and rain.

PATH OF HAIL STONES

COOL AIR

Inside the cloud warm air rises faster and faster. Then it cools and sinks.

Heavy rain begins to fall.

The wind blows. Tiny water drops get bigger and bigger.

RAIN

HAIL

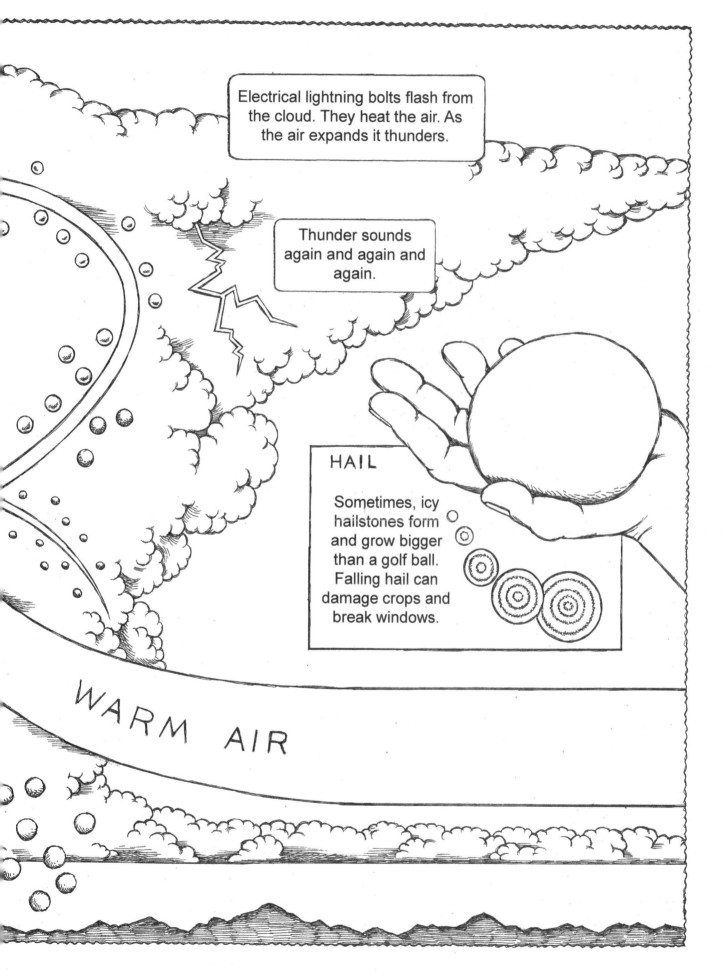

Electrical lightning bolts flash from the cloud. They heat the air. As the air expands it thunders.

Thunder sounds again and again and again.

HAIL

Sometimes, icy hailstones form and grow bigger than a golf ball. Falling hail can damage crops and break windows.

WARM AIR

RAINBOWS
Did you ever see a rainbow? Where did it come from? Where did it go?

Rainbows can appear when there is rain and the sun is shining. Sunlight that passes through the drops of rain bends and splits into colors.

RED
ORANGE
YELLOW
GREEN
BLUE
INDIGO
VIOLET

You can't reach a rainbow or touch it. It is only light in the sky.

When the sun moves or the rain stops, rainbows disappear.

For you to see a rainbow, the sun must be behind you and the rain in front of you.

If you shine white light through a prism, the light bends and splits into rainbow colors.

WHITE LIGHT

RED
ORANGE
YELLOW
GREEN
BLUE
INDIGO
VIOLET

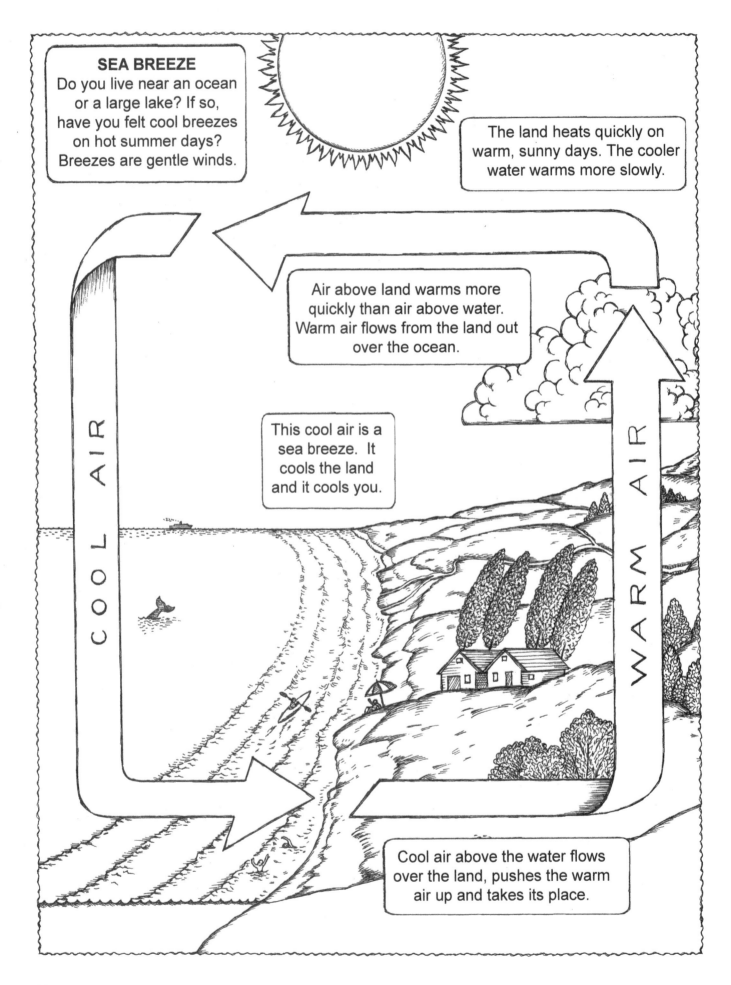

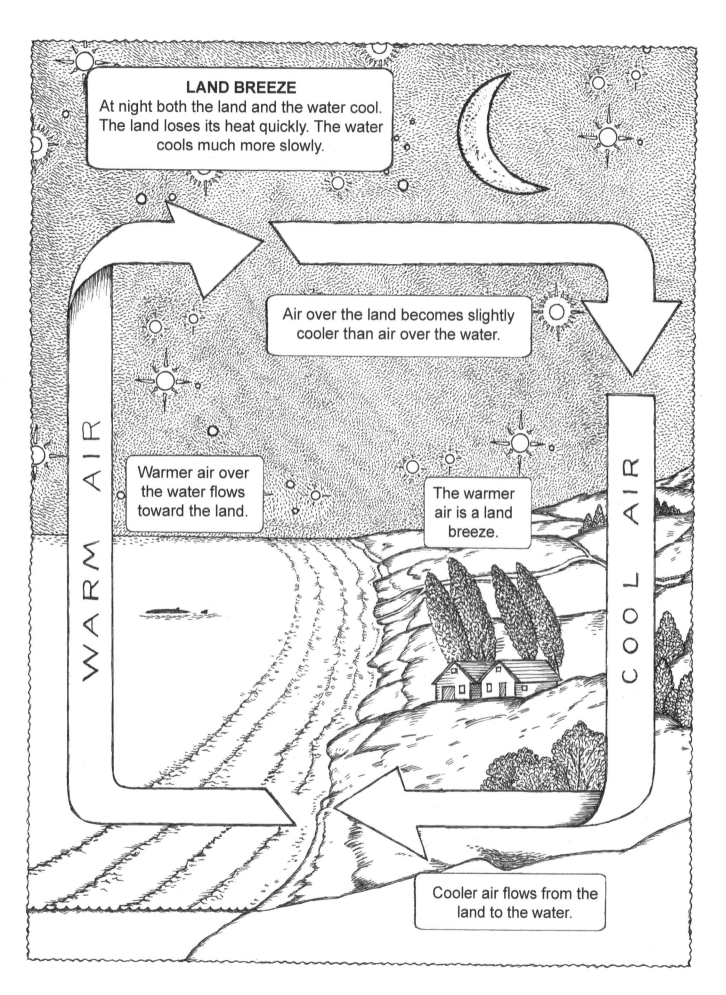

LAND BREEZE
At night both the land and the water cool. The land loses its heat quickly. The water cools much more slowly.

Air over the land becomes slightly cooler than air over the water.

Warmer air over the water flows toward the land.

The warmer air is a land breeze.

WARM AIR

COOL AIR

Cooler air flows from the land to the water.

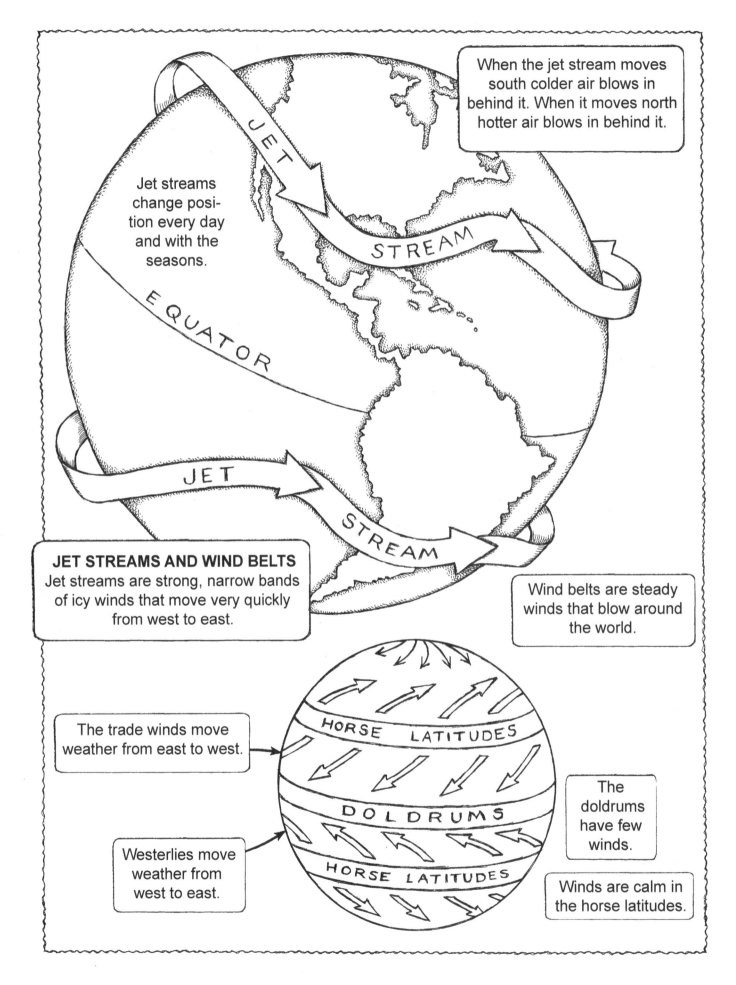

When the jet stream moves south colder air blows in behind it. When it moves north hotter air blows in behind it.

Jet streams change position every day and with the seasons.

JET STREAM

EQUATOR

JET STREAM

JET STREAMS AND WIND BELTS
Jet streams are strong, narrow bands of icy winds that move very quickly from west to east.

Wind belts are steady winds that blow around the world.

The trade winds move weather from east to west.

HORSE LATITUDES

DOLDRUMS

HORSE LATITUDES

The doldrums have few winds.

Westerlies move weather from west to east.

Winds are calm in the horse latitudes.

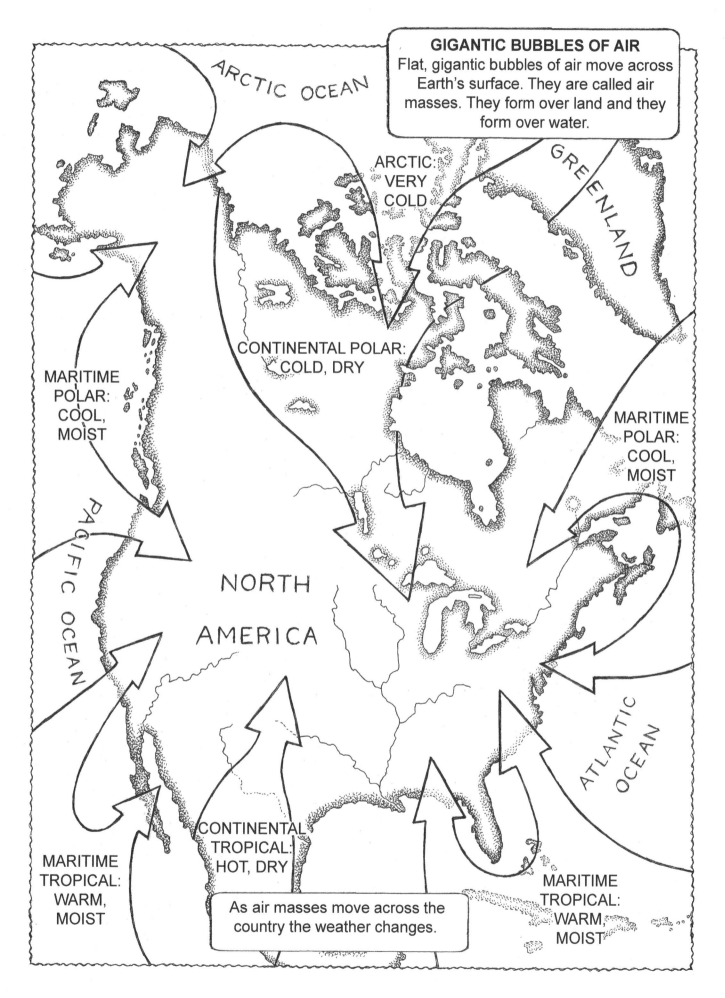

ARCTIC OCEAN

GIGANTIC BUBBLES OF AIR
Flat, gigantic bubbles of air move across
Earth's surface. They are called air
masses. They form over land and they
form over water.

ARCTIC:
VERY
COLD

GREENLAND

CONTINENTAL POLAR:
COLD, DRY

MARITIME
POLAR:
COOL,
MOIST

MARITIME
POLAR:
COOL,
MOIST

PACIFIC OCEAN

NORTH

AMERICA

ATLANTIC OCEAN

MARITIME
TROPICAL:
WARM,
MOIST

CONTINENTAL
TROPICAL:
HOT, DRY

As air masses move across the
country the weather changes.

MARITIME
TROPICAL:
WARM,
MOIST

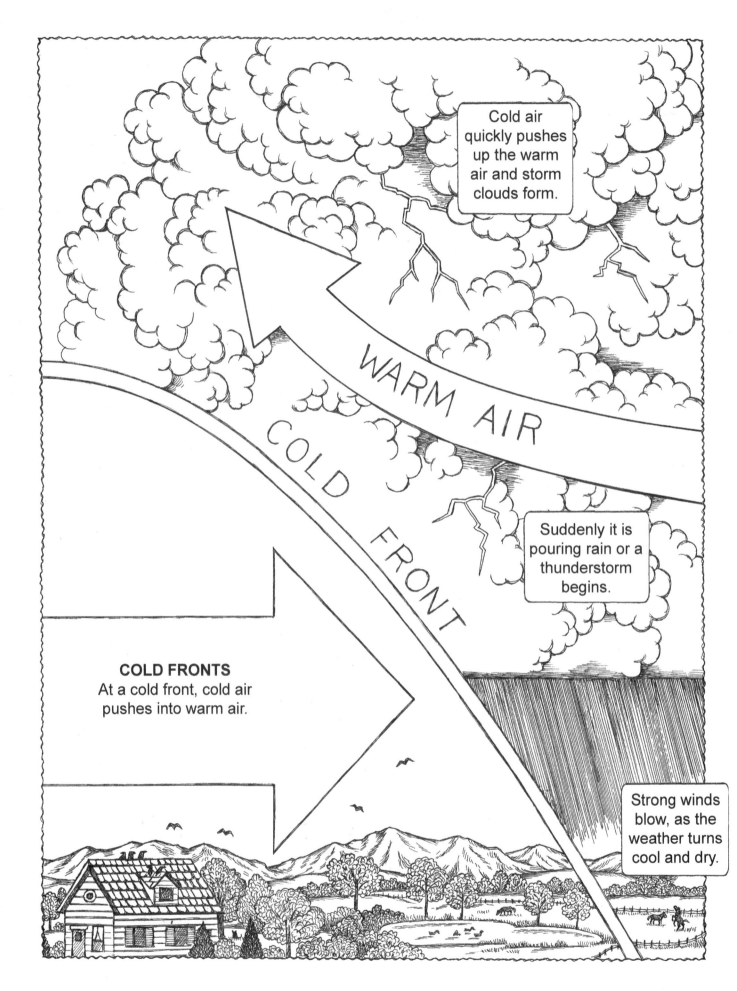

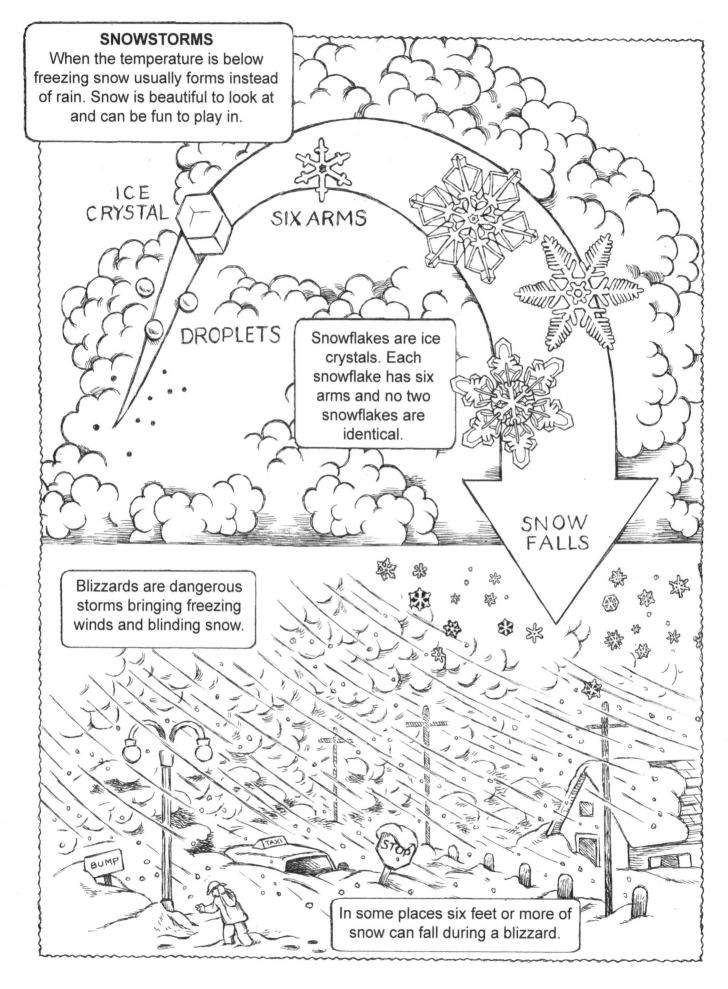

SNOWSTORMS
When the temperature is below freezing snow usually forms instead of rain. Snow is beautiful to look at and can be fun to play in.

ICE CRYSTAL

SIX ARMS

DROPLETS

Snowflakes are ice crystals. Each snowflake has six arms and no two snowflakes are identical.

SNOW FALLS

Blizzards are dangerous storms bringing freezing winds and blinding snow.

BUMP

TAXI

STOP

In some places six feet or more of snow can fall during a blizzard.

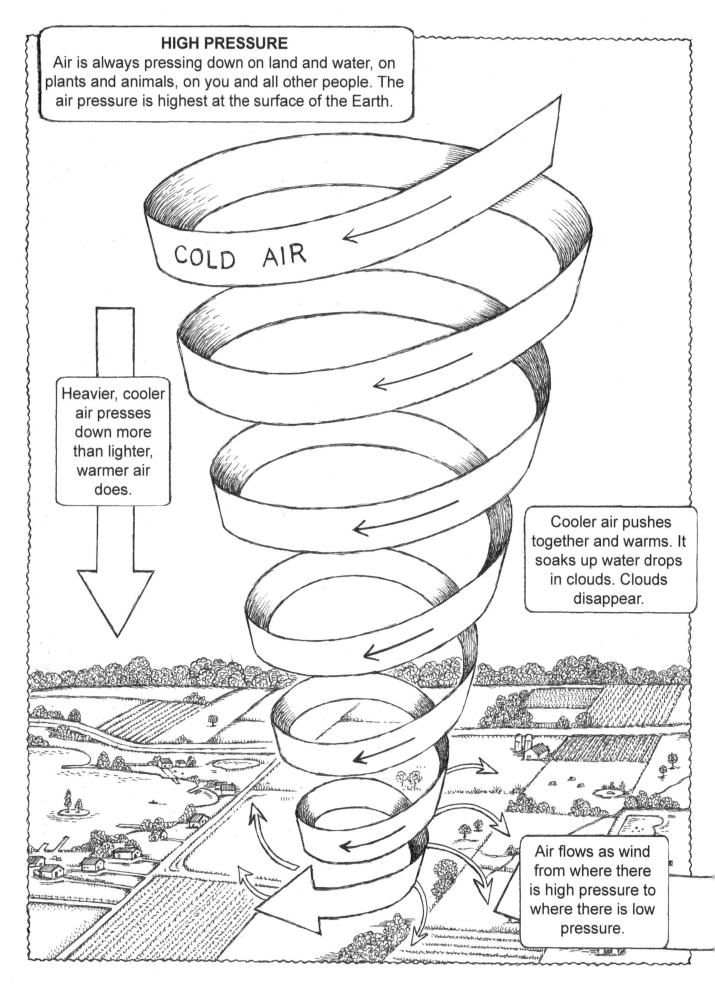

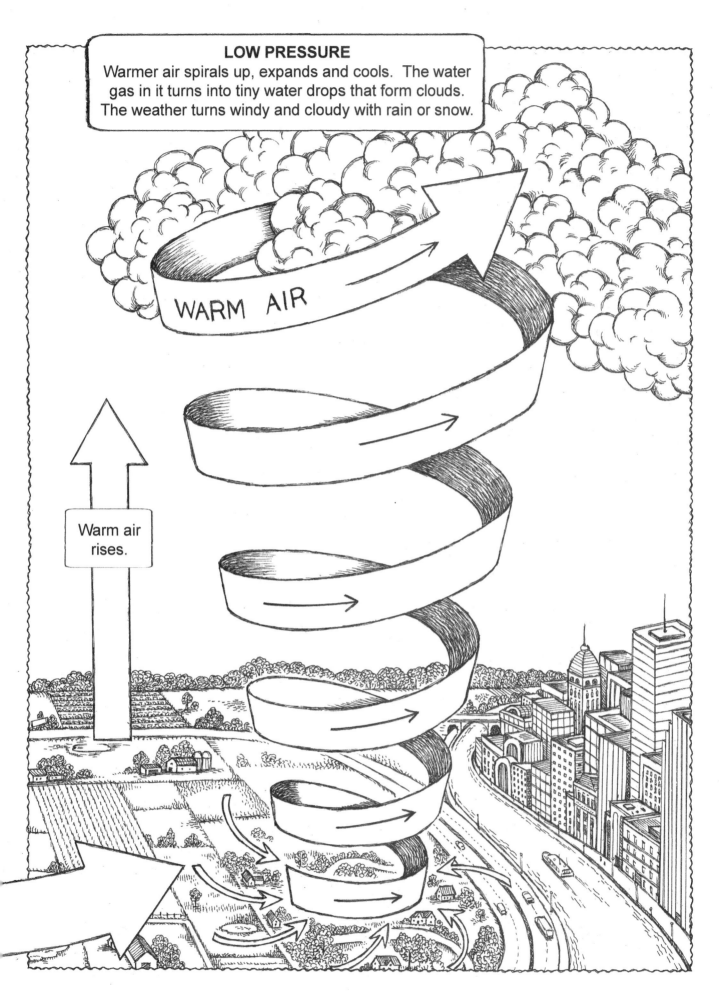

LOW PRESSURE
Warmer air spirals up, expands and cools. The water gas in it turns into tiny water drops that form clouds. The weather turns windy and cloudy with rain or snow.

WARM AIR

Warm air rises.

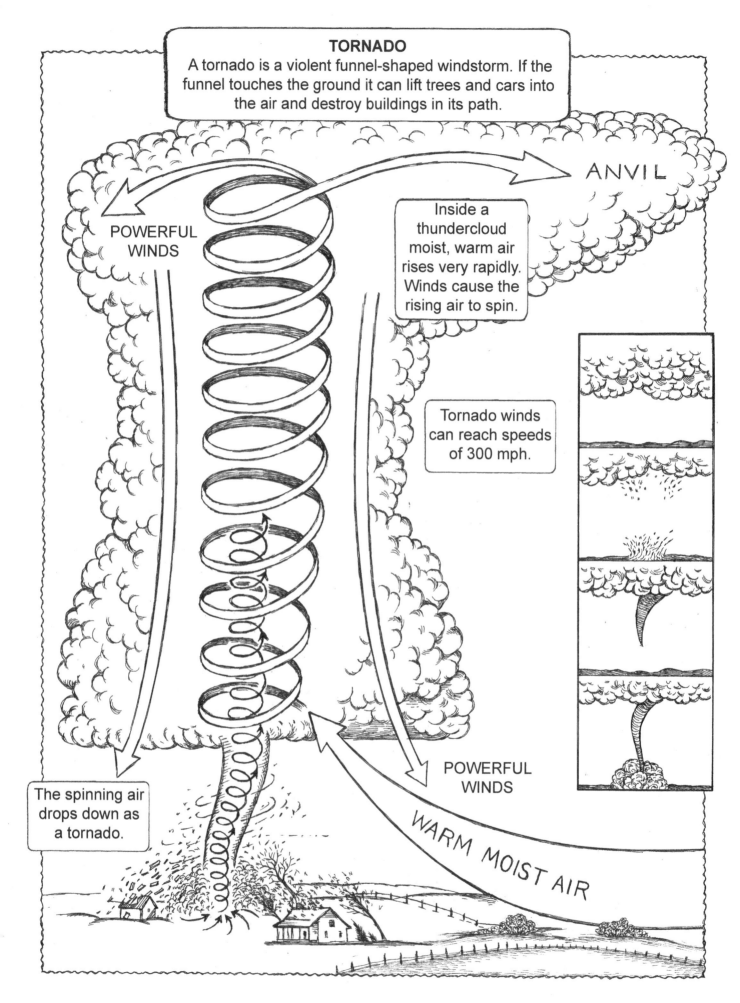

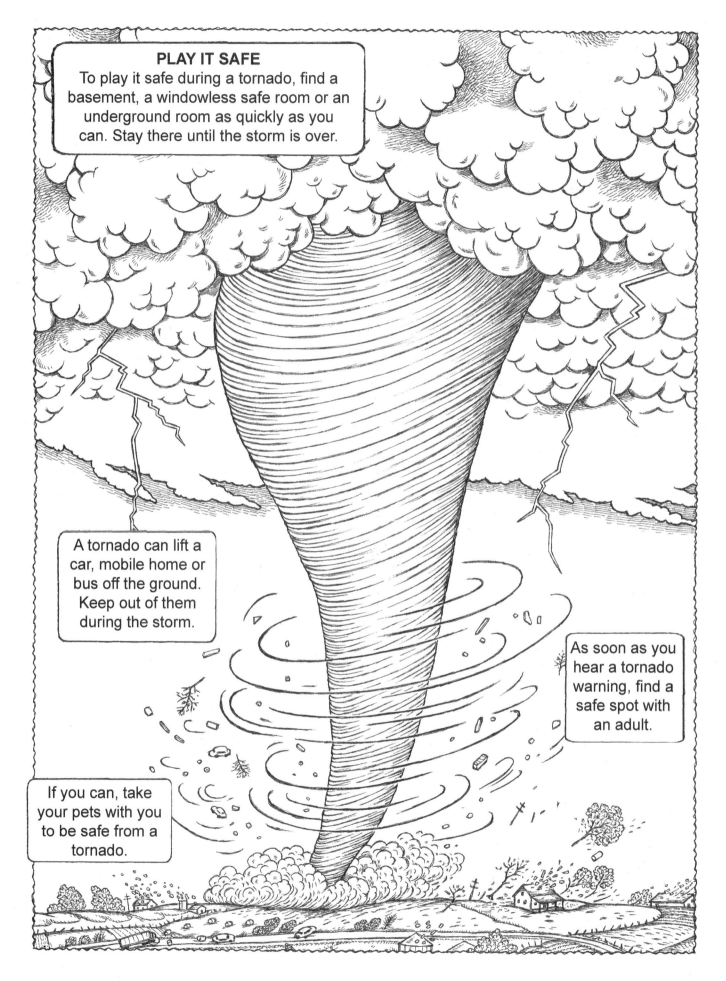

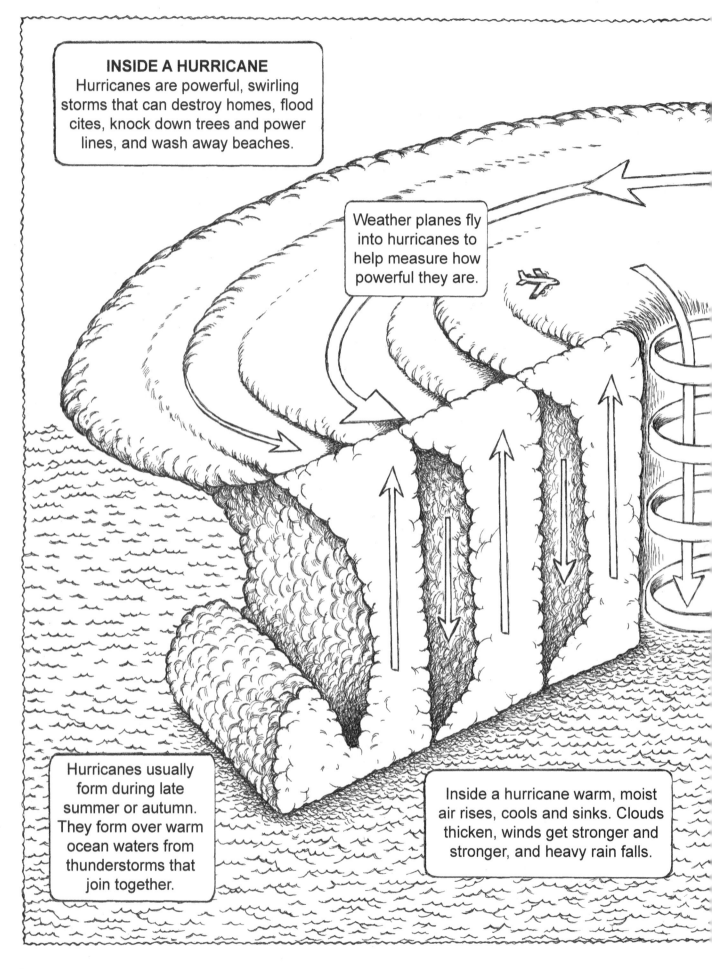

INSIDE A HURRICANE
Hurricanes are powerful, swirling storms that can destroy homes, flood cites, knock down trees and power lines, and wash away beaches.

Weather planes fly into hurricanes to help measure how powerful they are.

Hurricanes usually form during late summer or autumn. They form over warm ocean waters from thunderstorms that join together.

Inside a hurricane warm, moist air rises, cools and sinks. Clouds thicken, winds get stronger and stronger, and heavy rain falls.

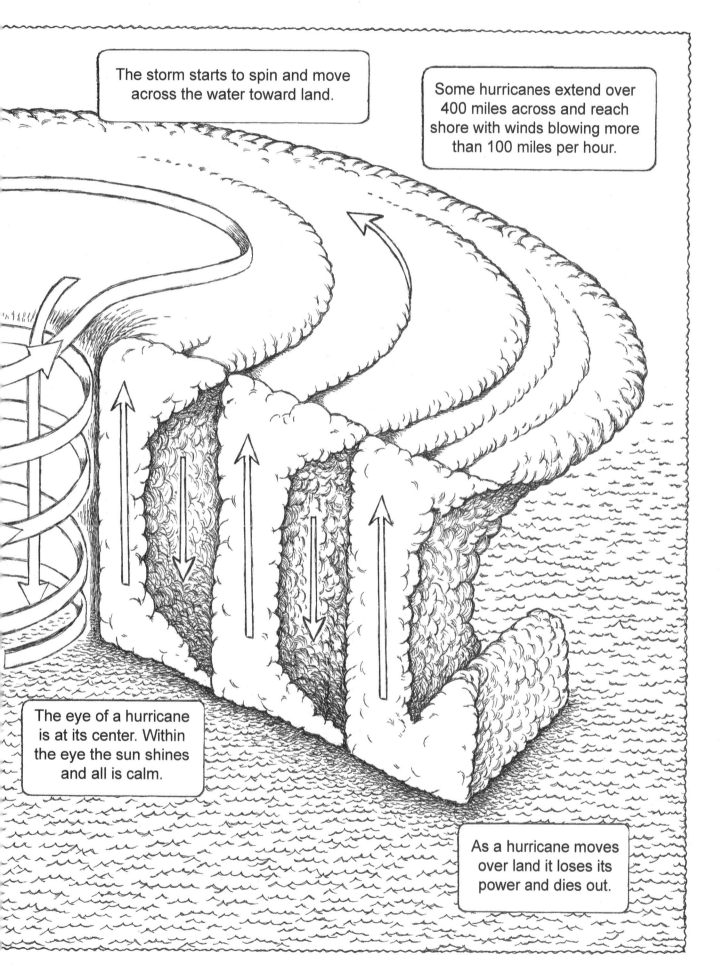

The storm starts to spin and move across the water toward land.

Some hurricanes extend over 400 miles across and reach shore with winds blowing more than 100 miles per hour.

The eye of a hurricane is at its center. Within the eye the sun shines and all is calm.

As a hurricane moves over land it loses its power and dies out.

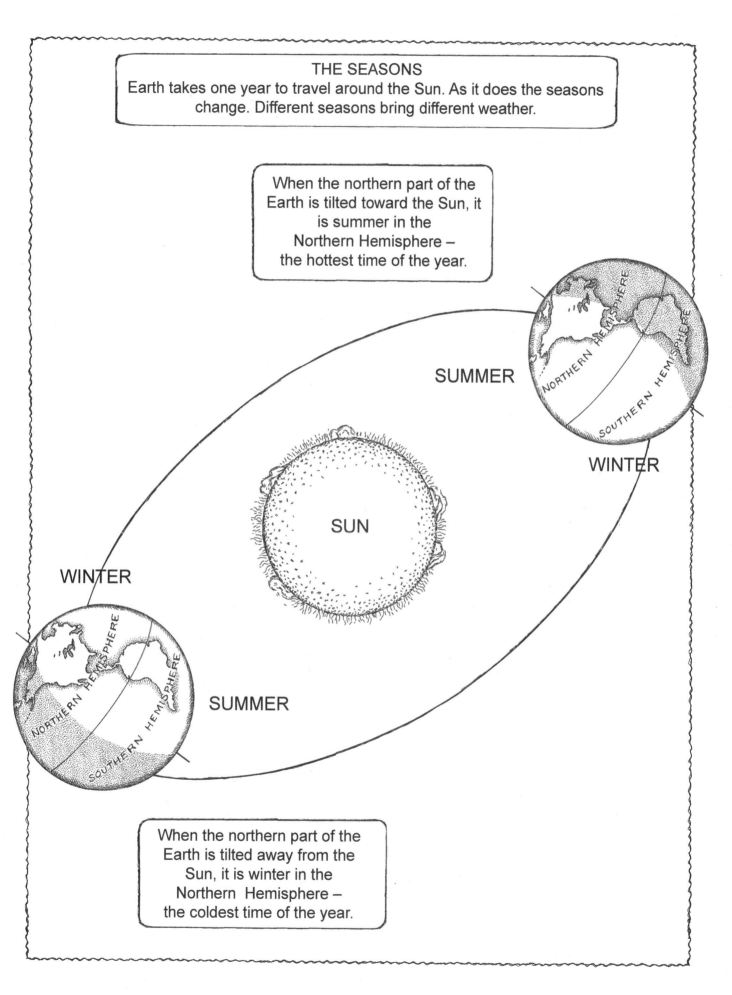

THE SEASONS
Earth takes one year to travel around the Sun. As it does the seasons change. Different seasons bring different weather.

When the northern part of the Earth is tilted toward the Sun, it is summer in the Northern Hemisphere – the hottest time of the year.

SUMMER

WINTER

SUN

NORTHERN HEMISPHERE

SOUTHERN HEMISPHERE

NORTHERN HEMISPHERE

SOUTHERN HEMISPHERE

WINTER

SUMMER

When the northern part of the Earth is tilted away from the Sun, it is winter in the Northern Hemisphere – the coldest time of the year.

SPRING
During spring, the days get longer. The air is warmer than in winter, but cooler than in summer.

On the first day of spring, day is as long as night.

In spring, winter ice melts and it often rains.

Trees bloom and flowers push up through the soil. Leaves start to grow.

Many animals have their young in spring.

Many plants bear fruits and seeds during summer.

SUMMER
The sun rises highest in the sky during summer. Summer days are longer than summer nights. In many places days are hot and nights are warm.

Plants grow and grow during summer. There is plenty of food for most animals and their young.

31

AUTUMN
During autumn, the days get shorter and the nights longer. The weather is cooler than in summer but warmer than in winter.

Some autumn nights get so cold that frost forms.

In autumn, the green leaves of many plants turn color as they die and fall. Most plants store food in their roots and stems for winter.

Many birds and some butterflies fly hundreds, even thousands of miles, to places where winter is warm.

WINTER
In winter the sun does not rise high in the sky.

Winter days are shorter than winter nights. In many places the weather turns so cold that ice forms.

It often snows in winter.

Many animals sleep, or hibernate, during the winter. Few plants keep their leaves during cold winters.

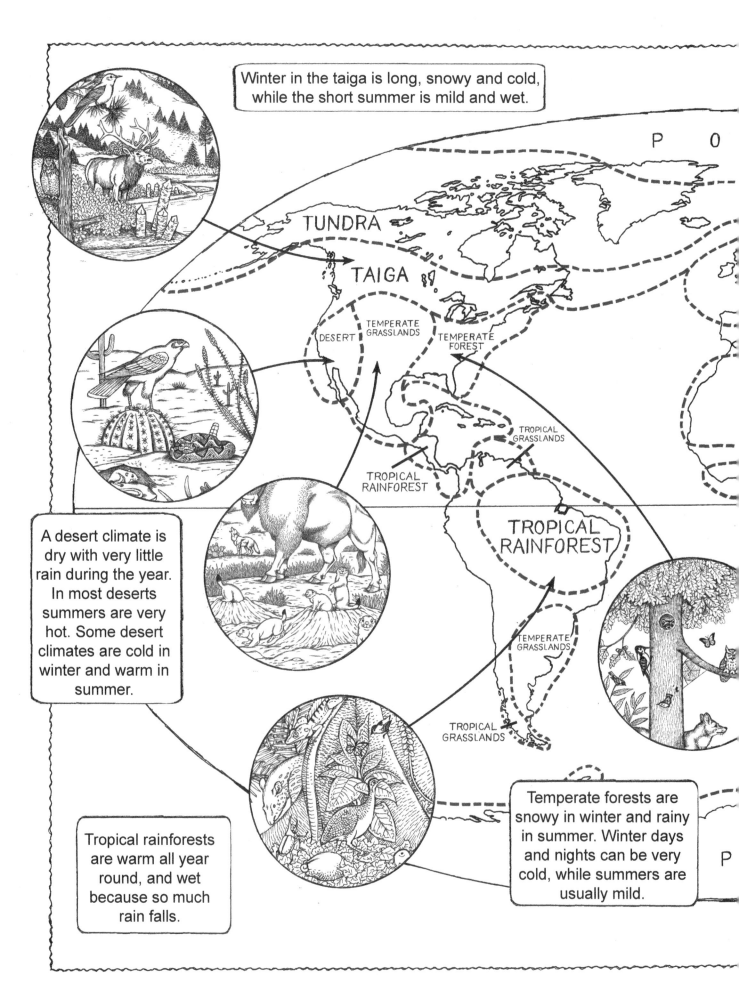

Winter in the taiga is long, snowy and cold, while the short summer is mild and wet.

P O

TUNDRA

TAIGA

DESERT

TEMPERATE GRASSLANDS

TEMPERATE FOREST

TROPICAL GRASSLANDS

TROPICAL RAINFOREST

TROPICAL RAINFOREST

TEMPERATE GRASSLANDS

TROPICAL GRASSLANDS

A desert climate is dry with very little rain during the year. In most deserts summers are very hot. Some desert climates are cold in winter and warm in summer.

Tropical rainforests are warm all year round, and wet because so much rain falls.

Temperate forests are snowy in winter and rainy in summer. Winter days and nights can be very cold, while summers are usually mild.

P

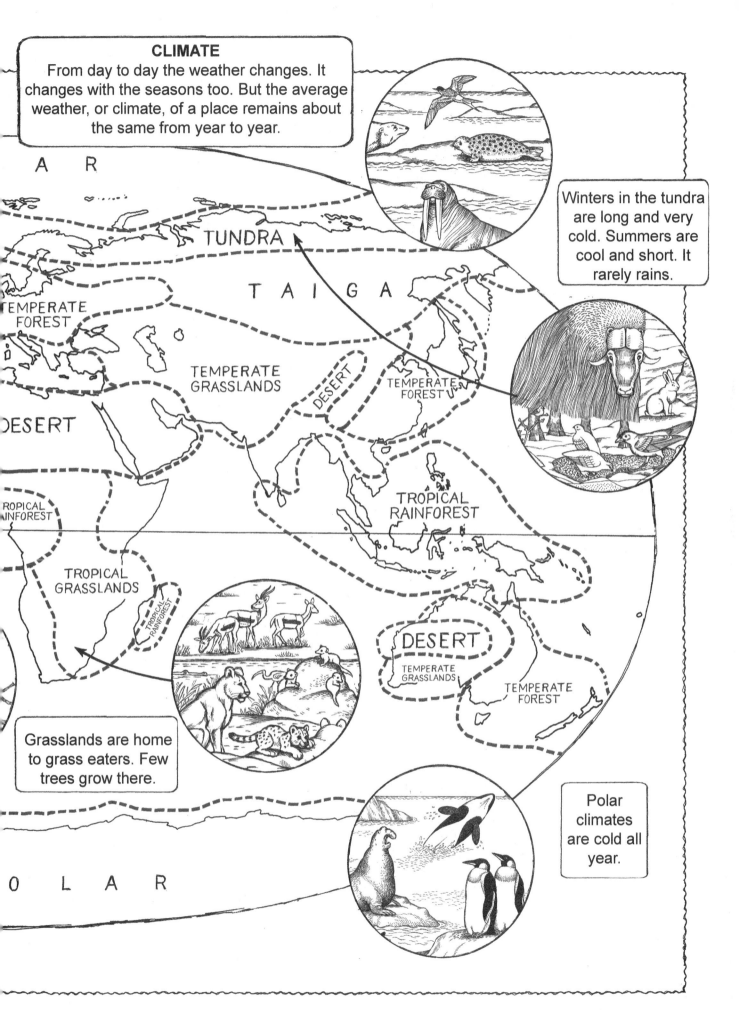

CLIMATE
From day to day the weather changes. It changes with the seasons too. But the average weather, or climate, of a place remains about the same from year to year.

A   R

TUNDRA

T A I G A

TEMPERATE FOREST

Winters in the tundra are long and very cold. Summers are cool and short. It rarely rains.

TEMPERATE GRASSLANDS

DESERT

TEMPERATE FOREST

DESERT

ROPICAL INFOREST

TROPICAL RAINFOREST

TROPICAL GRASSLANDS

TROPICAL RAINFOREST

DESERT

TEMPERATE GRASSLANDS

TEMPERATE FOREST

Grasslands are home to grass eaters. Few trees grow there.

Polar climates are cold all year.

O   L A R

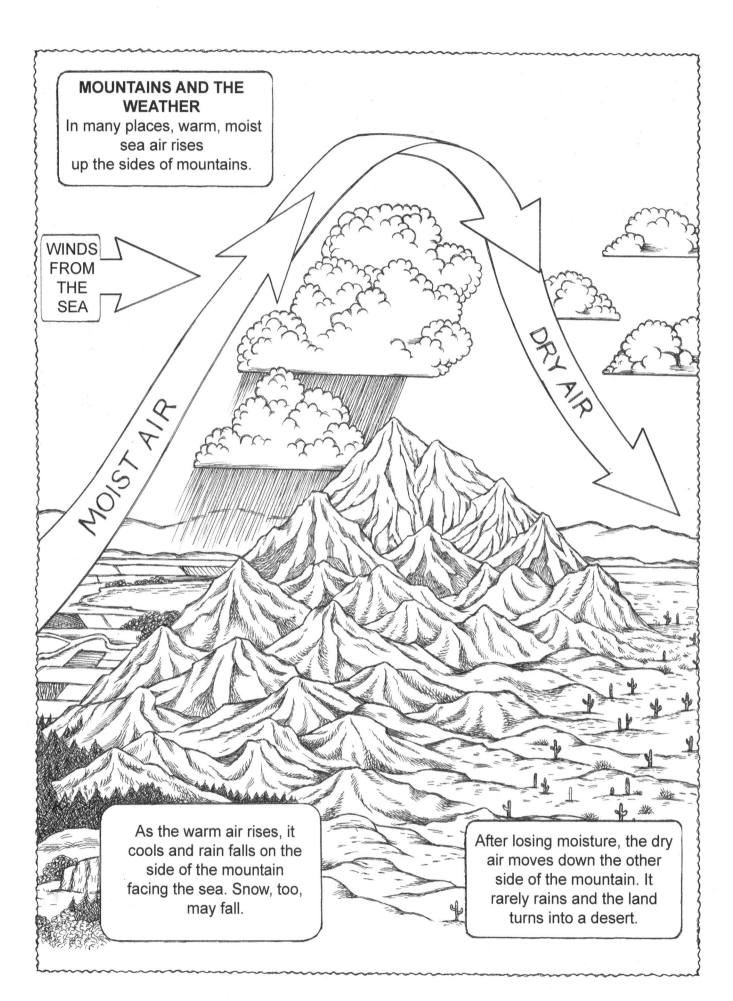

MOUNTAINS AND THE WEATHER
In many places, warm, moist sea air rises up the sides of mountains.

WINDS FROM THE SEA

MOIST AIR

DRY AIR

As the warm air rises, it cools and rain falls on the side of the mountain facing the sea. Snow, too, may fall.

After losing moisture, the dry air moves down the other side of the mountain. It rarely rains and the land turns into a desert.

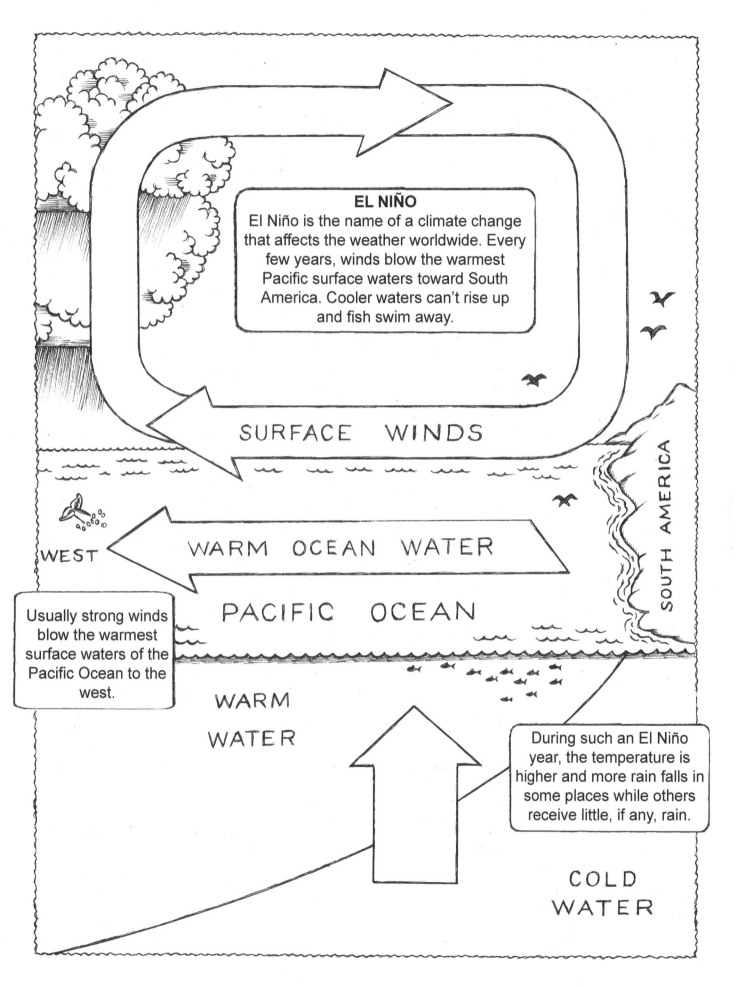

SINKHOLES AND MUDSLIDES
Imagine a hole that appears in the ground and swallows up a car or even a house. Sound crazy? Not to people who live in places where sinkholes form.

Heavy rain or snow that melts quickly can cause a mudslide. Tons of mud can carry away trees, rocks, cars, and homes.

During a heavy rainfall a large sinkhole can open on a road or in a backyard, even under a house.

Sinkholes form when rain fills cracks in limestone and slowly eats away the stone.

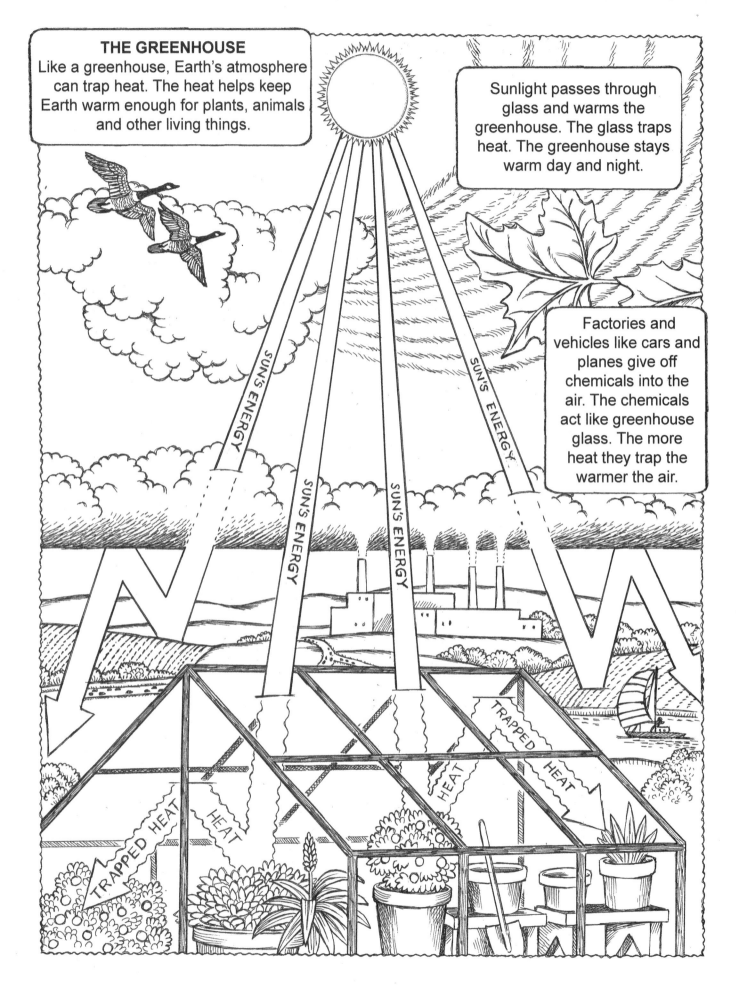

THE GREENHOUSE
Like a greenhouse, Earth's atmosphere can trap heat. The heat helps keep Earth warm enough for plants, animals and other living things.

Sunlight passes through glass and warms the greenhouse. The glass traps heat. The greenhouse stays warm day and night.

Factories and vehicles like cars and planes give off chemicals into the air. The chemicals act like greenhouse glass. The more heat they trap the warmer the air.

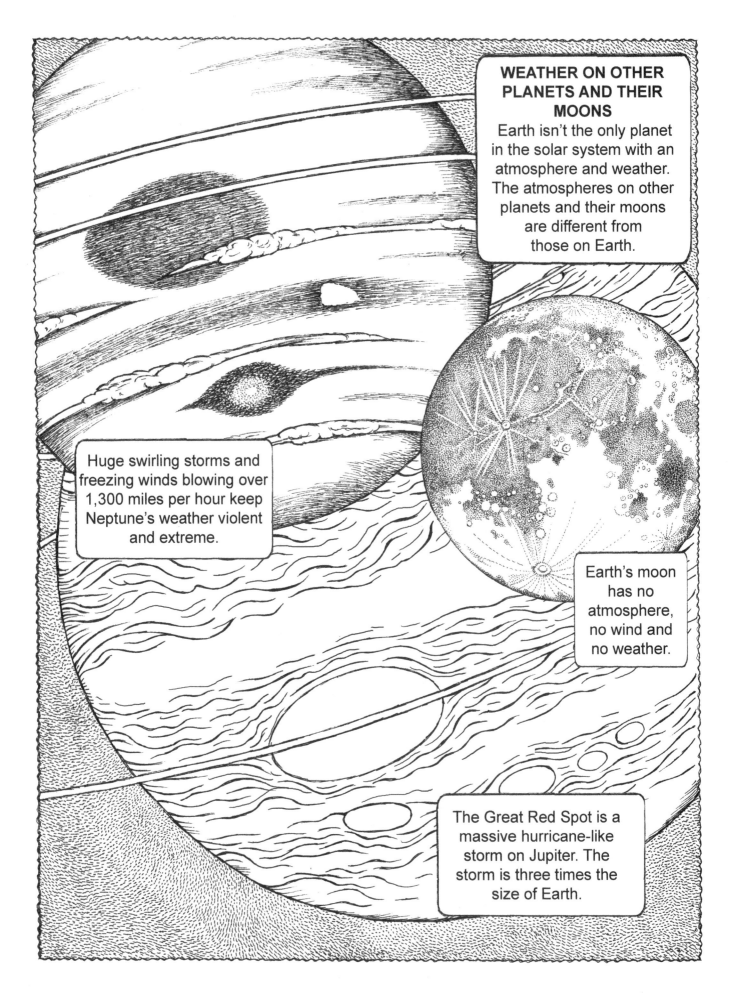

WEATHER ON OTHER PLANETS AND THEIR MOONS
Earth isn't the only planet in the solar system with an atmosphere and weather. The atmospheres on other planets and their moons are different from those on Earth.

Huge swirling storms and freezing winds blowing over 1,300 miles per hour keep Neptune's weather violent and extreme.

Earth's moon has no atmosphere, no wind and no weather.

The Great Red Spot is a massive hurricane-like storm on Jupiter. The storm is three times the size of Earth.

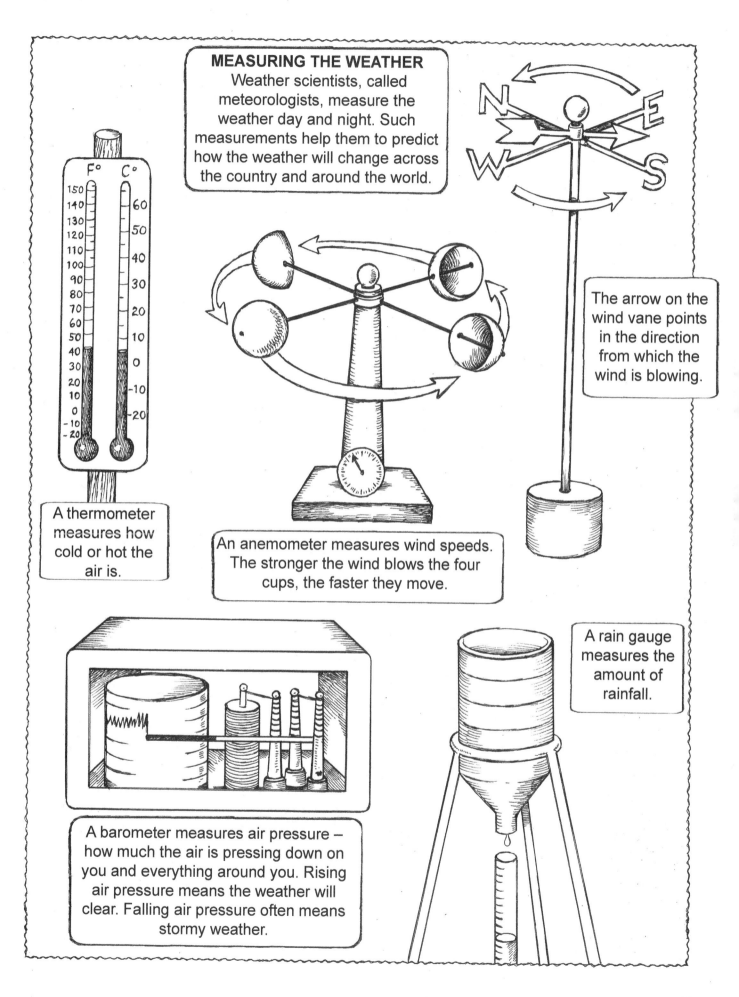

MEASURING THE WEATHER
Weather scientists, called meteorologists, measure the weather day and night. Such measurements help them to predict how the weather will change across the country and around the world.

The arrow on the wind vane points in the direction from which the wind is blowing.

A thermometer measures how cold or hot the air is.

An anemometer measures wind speeds. The stronger the wind blows the four cups, the faster they move.

A rain gauge measures the amount of rainfall.

A barometer measures air pressure – how much the air is pressing down on you and everything around you. Rising air pressure means the weather will clear. Falling air pressure often means stormy weather.

MAPPING THE WEATHER

Did you ever hear a weather report? It predicts, or forecasts, what the weather will be for the rest of the day, the next day, and even a week after that.

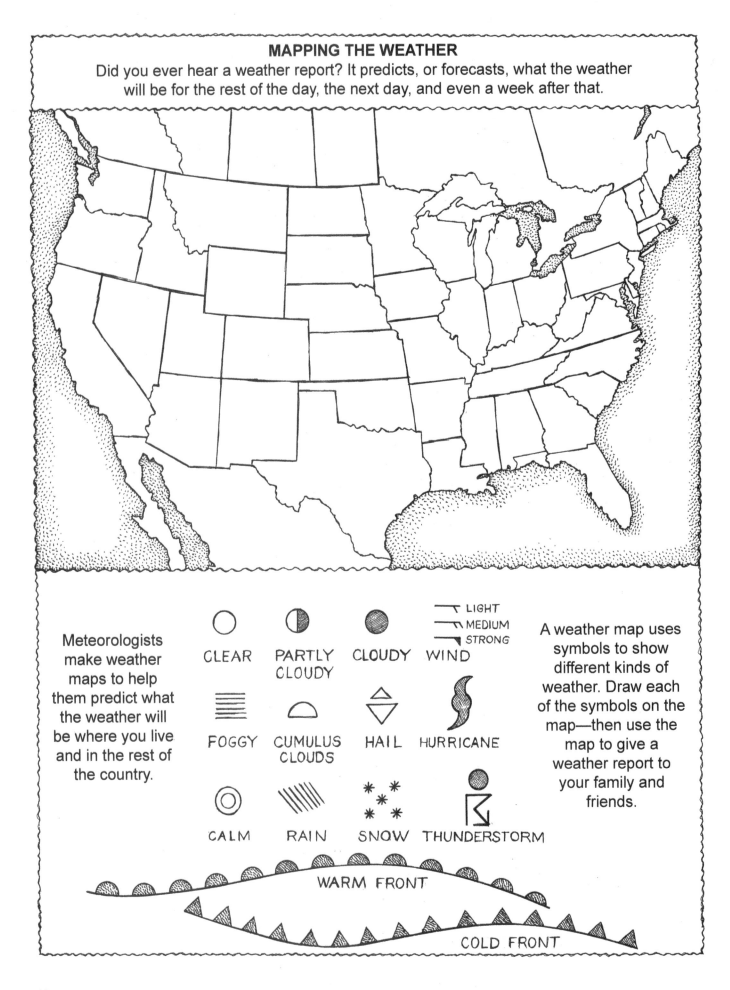

Meteorologists make weather maps to help them predict what the weather will be where you live and in the rest of the country.

CLEAR PARTLY CLOUDY CLOUDY WIND — LIGHT / MEDIUM / STRONG

FOGGY CUMULUS CLOUDS HAIL HURRICANE

CALM RAIN SNOW THUNDERSTORM

A weather map uses symbols to show different kinds of weather. Draw each of the symbols on the map—then use the map to give a weather report to your family and friends.

WARM FRONT

COLD FRONT